T0149105

LIGHT Or r WATER

LIGHT OFF WATER

XXV Catalan Poems
1978–2002

Edited by Iolanda Pelegrí with Anna Crowe

CARCANET

SCOTTISH POETRY LIBRARY

By leaves we live

First published in 2007 by

The Scottish Poetry Library
5 Crichton's Close
Canongate
Edinburgh
EH8 8DT

and

Carcanet Press Limited
Alliance House
Cross Street
Manchester
M2 7AQ

Introduction and this selection © 2007 Iolanda Pelegrí
Editorial concept © 2004 Scottish Poetry Library
Individual poems © the authors and translators; the acknowledgements on p. 90
constitute an extension of this copyright page.

ISBN 1 85754 916 3

The publishers gratefully acknowledge support from the Institut Ramon Llull
(Catalunya), the Scottish Arts Council and the Tom Wright Memorial Fund towards the
publication of this title.

Designed and typeset by Barrie Tullett in Shaker

Printed and bound by
Wayzgoose of Lincoln, UK

Contents

Editorial Note

This selection was made on the principle of one poem per year. The poem may have appeared in a magazine or a collection published during that year. Publication details appear with the poets' biographies at the end of the book.

I would like to extend my thanks to everyone involved in this publication, particularly Iolanda Pelegrí who accepted the challenge of choosing twenty-five poems; the translators Anna Crowe and Christopher Whyte for their creative responses, and to Anna for her enabling role; the Institut Ramon Llull (Catalunya) for its encouragement and support; to Eilidh Bateman at the Scottish Poetry Library and those at Carcanet Press who have helped to bring this project to fruition.

We do not anticipate publishing more volumes in this series, although the format offers infinite possibilities. It was a simple dream yet very complicated in execution, and I have been heartened by the warm response from readers, poets, and translators in Scotland and the European countries involved. It suggests that curiosity and creativity, which the Scottish Poetry Library exists to satisfy and nurture, powers the two-way poetic traffic of Scotland in Europe and Europe in Scotland.

Robyn Marsack
Series Editor

Introduction

When it rains I dance alone
Dressed in algae, gold and fishscales.
There's a stretch of sea at turning
And a patch of scarlet sky
[...]
When I sleep, then I see clearly
Crazed by a sweet poison.

*J.V.Foix**

These lines are the beginning and end of one of the best-known poems by the surrealist poet, J.V. Foix (1893-1987). A poem dated April 1939, when General Franco had won the war (Barcelona had fallen at the end of January) and put in place the policy of prohibition and persecution of the Catalan language and, consequently, of its literature. Poets, therefore, had been cut off, with no opportunity of communicating with their readers. In spite of this extremely negative state of affairs, Foix and many other writers continued to write in their own language, and in their search for the dream (or being '[c]razed') tried to 'rescue words for yourselves' as Salvador Espriu (1913-85) urged later - another of the poets who never left Catalonia. Those who had to go into exile wanted to make sure that Catalan literature survived, publishing books and magazines in those countries where they had taken refuge, so that during the first years of the Franco dictatorship more books were published in Catalan in South America than in Catalonia.

*Translated by David H. Rosenthal in J.V.Foix, *When I Sleep, then I See Clearly* (New York: Persea Books, 1988).

Many of the poets in this anthology were young people or children during the war, while others were educated during the grey, repressive post-war years, growing up with the idealised image of the government of the *Generalitat* of the Republican era (1931-39), when Catalan language and literature enjoyed full normality.

Of the twenty-five poets selected, five – Agustí Bartra (1908), Joan Vinyoli (1914), Josep Palau i Fabre (1917), Montserrat Abelló (1918), and Joan Brossa (1919) – were young when the Civil War broke out. Bartra, Vinyoli and Palau i Fabre took an active part in literary life. They, together with writers such as Espriu (one of the best-known poets of the post-war period and the most widely translated) and Joan Teixidor, constitute the so-called 'sacrificed generation': the generation who saw their literary careers cut short and who suffered physical or internal exile.

Agustí Bartra, who was a soldier, had to flee to France where at first he was interned in a concentration camp, then finally transferred to Roissy-en-Brie, a village not far from Paris where a group of Catalan writers had taken refuge. At Roissy he met the writer Anna Murià, with whom he shared the rest of his life. A life-affirming and pantheistic poet, admirer of Walt Whitman, faithful to his idea of the poet's role as his destiny, Bartra went on writing up to a few months before he died. Significantly, it is to his wife that he dedicates some of these poems. One, 'Anna Sleeps', springing from his pain and illness, is a song full of hope, to this love of more than forty years.

Meanwhile, the poets who had remained in the Spanish state or who had returned quite early on – such as Carles Riba (1893-1959) – lived in 'internal exile', particularly hard until 1945 when, after the defeat of the Fascist regimes, a chink of permissiveness began to emerge. Palau i Fabre had to publish his first work clandestinely (1943), and Vinyoli, who had published his first book in 1937, did not publish his second until 1948; some of the books that Brossa wrote during this period remain unpublished. By means of various aesthetic routes, the poets attempted to safeguard the language and stay in touch with their own tradition: in Vinyoli's case, along the line closest to symbolism, while Palau and Brossa became involved with avant-garde movements related to surrealism. Both Palau and Brossa were active members of the literary resistance: the former organised poetry readings and was the moving force behind the magazine *Poesia* (1944-45), while the latter was one of the founders of the magazine *Dau al Set* (1948).

The poetry of Joan Vinyoli, with its debt to German romanticism and post-symbolism, has a metaphysical and existential edge, and for him poetry is the only path to salvation for the human condition. He himself defined it as 'realist-existentialist'. His is a profound poetry, devoid of artifice, characteristics which become more clearly defined with the publication of his collection *Cercles* (1979) in which nature, and the sea in particular, is a pretext for meditating on self-knowledge, life and death.

Josep Palau i Fabre, who lived in France from 1945 until 1961, considered poetry to be 'alchemy, that is to say: the immediate and chaotic experimentation of life on paper, the opposite of chemistry'. Thus, for him, it is a radical act resulting in transformation. From his youth a reader of Rimbaud (whom he translated into Catalan) and of the medieval Catalan writer Ramon Llull (whom he translated into French), Palau i Fabre knew Antonin Artaud, and was a close friend of Picasso, to whom he dedicated his dramatic work *Homenatge a Picasso*. This recreates some of Picasso's paintings, among them, *Guernica*, which inspired the poem chosen here.

Likewise a translator of Rimbaud, the avant-garde poet Joan Brossa considered poetry to be an act of investigation and research, having at the same time a collective dimension: it constitutes a socio-political denunciation of reality and reveals a different way of looking at the world. In his last books, there is a more metaphysical perception at work, reflecting on life and death, evident in the collection, *Passat festes/After the holidays* (1995). In the poem 'Plain Sonnet', he enquires into the poet's role and reveals his intention of working right up to the end, which he did.

Born before the Civil War, too young to take an active part but old enough to remember it, Blai Bonet, Jordi Sarsanedas, Miquel Martí i Pol and Feliu Formosa all suffered the repressive atmosphere of the immediate post-war period, an atmosphere in which Joan Margarit, born in 1938, grew up. From the 1950s onwards, Catalan literature began to return to relative normality and to have a presence, although very faint, in the publishing world. In the face of cultural oppression, poetry became a weapon with which to combat the Franco dictatorship and achieve the liberation of the human spirit. Following the theories of Gramsci and Lukács, Catalan critics advocated a literature that was close to social reality, written in accessible and direct language.

Jordi Sarsanedas' civic and aesthetic attitudes make him a very demanding poet. On his return from France, he was an active participant in movements of cultural renewal, but his writing is difficult to classify. An admirer of the avant-garde poet Joan Salvat-Papasseït (1894-1924), Sarsanedas employs very abstract themes and symbols alongside readymade phrases and images belonging to everyday speech, with great control of language (both of the meaning of words and their sounds), rhythm and syntax.

Although for those living in Mallorca the war situation was different, since the rebel soldiers had triumphed with very little resistance, the repression was very severe, as reflected in some of Blai Bonet's work. A provocative and cultured poet, the weight of his religious education is evident in his work and in his imagery, in which the use of colour is very important. Water, rocks and plants are the protagonists in 'The most beautiful kind of Catalan in the world', a title which looks back to the nineteenth century, when Catalan began to recover its status as a literary language. At the end of the poem, the poet concludes that the language is as alive as the magic flower that grows close to the ground, that is to say, close to the people.

Like Bonet the son of working-class parents, though in this case from the plain of Vic, Martí i Pol began working in a factory at the age of fourteen, and remained there until he was forty-three when he had to retire because of illness. Martí i Pol writes 'because he enjoys it' and in order to question reality. From early works grounded in historical realism, such as *La fàbrica* (1972), Martí i Pol's poetry became more reflective and intimate with the onset of illness, and especially after the death of his first wife. In his final years he reflected on the approach of death while weighing up his own life.

At the end of the 1960s and during the 1970s there appeared on the literary scene the 'seventies generation', writers born between 1940 and 1950, who wanted to create a different aesthetic from that of the prevailing historic realism. Seven of the anthologised poets – Miquel Bauçà, Narcís Comadira, Francesc Parcerisas, Pere Gimferrer, Damià Huguet, Jaume Pont and Maria Mercé Marçal – all share, at the very least, this aesthetic impulse, even though the early publications of some of these writers should be classed as historic realism. They assert, on the one hand, the autonomy of the act of writing and the importance of technical and formal aspects, while, at the same time, influenced by Gabriel Ferrater (1922-72), aiming for a poetry more closely related to individual experience rather than to the description of society. Educated in Spanish, they had to discover the literary models of their own tradition, and reclaim poets of the avant-garde, such as J.V. Foix or Brossa, and poets with connections to symbolism such as J. Carner and Vinyoli. They wished to make their voices heard, creating publishing houses and poetry magazines.

In his book, *Terra natal* (1978), Narcís Comadira has written a brief, highly significant poem about his perception of the historical and literary situation that we may take to include the whole of his generation:

Question

Defeat is my inheritance,
Confusion is my present,
Sadness everything to come.
In spite of all I still wonder:
Shall I be done with praising**?**

In the face of this question, Comadira, like the other poets already referred to, replies with his dedication to literature and to art. Both in *Terra natal / Native Land* and in *Album de familia / Family Album*, he reflects on historical and family circumstances, on love, life and death. Death in 'Blue Irises' unites nature at its most fragile, represented by the iris, with humanity at its most fragile, the children killed by the bombs of the German Luftwaffe in Guernica during the Spanish Civil War.

Although some critics considered the first books of the Mallorcan poet Miquel Bauçà to have been written in a style of existentialist realism, Bauçà's aesthetic road has always been highly personal. Like many poets, he asks himself what the poet is. The reply is atypical of Catalan poetry, for the poet is neither the voice of the people, nor an alchemist, nor a privileged being; the poet is the same as everyone else, and poetry has a therapeutic effect: 'While poetry may not eradicate the disease, while it may not eradicate the problem**,** it does not mean that it may not be an analgesic. And at the same time, a tool – the only one we have in confronting Evil.'

Likewise from Mallorca, six years younger than Bauçà, Damià Huguet set up a poetry publishing house, Guaret, where he published some of his own books and works by other writers. A friend of Blai Bonet, who strongly influenced his early work, he writes long, discursive poems with a broken syntax. The explorer of diverse poetic paths, he investigates love, passion, sex, the cinema, writing, and the destruction of the Mallorcan landscape, drowned in concrete.

The title of Francesc Parcerisas's first book, *Vint poemes civils / Twenty civilian poems* (1967), signals the social purpose that has provoked his poetry. But lately, Parcerisas, influenced by Gabriel Ferrater and by English poets such as W. H Auden, is evolving towards a poetry where the experience of daily life is transcended by reflections on love, passion, and the importance of art in capturing the moment and arresting the inevitable passing of time, as is clearly shown in the poem here, 'The Egyptian Room'.

Writing and art as a meta-theme is a constant in the work of Pere Gimferrer, who sees poetry as a reflection in distorting mirrors, and art and literature as a world with its own autonomy. In the poem, 'Words for a stonecutter', in homage to Joan Miró, nature in its broad sense is immortalised thanks to the art of the painter and to the language – which is likewise an art – of Gimferrer. In a baroque poem, rich in imagery with its collage technique and juxtaposition of phrases, the poet introduces us to a world full of colours (green, earth-coloured, ruddy), of senses (touch, sight, hearing), of fire (sun, lightning), earth and water, which recall paintings by Miró.

For the Lleidan poet, Jaume Pont, 'poetry is a form of knowledge which makes visible what cannot be seen or, conversely, places the most conventional dictates of reality in contradiction until they dissolve'. In its formal aspect, Jaume Pont's poetry is based on the use of powerful images where opposites come into play (as in Paul Celan's work) and polarise: light and shadow, fire and ash, love and death. Death, specifically that of his father, is the mainspring of the book, *Vol de cendres / Flight of ashes* (1996), a work written out of grief and love. 'The Angel of Death' concludes the first part of this single-minded and poignant collection.

The youngest poet of this generation is also from Lleida, Maria Mercè Marçal, one of the most original Catalan poetic voices. She has a great command of language and of the lyric sources, images and symbols related to traditional poetry and folktales. Love is the motive of the sonnet featured here, a love between a woman and a man which needs a series of transformations in order to exist since, as the writer herself says, 'In order for love between a woman and a man to become possible, it seems as though a kind of inversion of the whole context is required', an inversion which affects nature also. The poem's images are drawn from popular traditional poetry, combined with surrealist elements that have echoes of Lorca.

Although Feliu Formosa published his first book in the 1970s, he is older than the poets previously mentioned, and he does not consider himself to be part of the generation of the seventies. A deeply reflective writer, his poetry is full of cultural references and is framed by literary landscapes. *Semblança / Likeness* is a good example of this: the poet spells out in fifteen poems (all sharing the same structure) an amorous journey that goes from separation to union, attained in poem VIII and celebrated in the final poems. The landscape, especially water, is the backcloth to this union and of the feelings it engenders.

The Lleidan poet Joan Margarit published his first book in Catalan in 1981, a collection which was well received in literary circles. Margarit searches for harmony between the human, the world and language. One of his most significant books is *Edat Roja*, the age of the poet's maturity, in which the marine landscape is the protagonist and symbol of life and, at the same time, of death. In his poem 'Post-scriptum', Margarit vindicates poetry as a medium for perpetuating memory and love in the search for the treasure island (the impossible ideal) necessary for survival.

That same year, Montserrat Abelló, then in her sixties, published her second collection, *Paraules no dites / Unuttered words*. This title and that of her first book, *Vida diària / Daily Life*, are mottoes for her poetry: on the one hand, a poetry where the most uncompromising and utterly everyday, made of simple gestures, is turned into lyric material and, on the other, a tool by which to leave silence behind and bring into the open words smothered by a world in which women have to struggle to make their voices heard. In this sense, both Maria Mercè Marçal and Montserrat Abelló are leaders of the feminist movements which sprang up in Catalonia at the end of the 1970s.

During the 1980s, an empty space was created in Catalonia by the death of many of the literary figures already referred to: in 1982 Agustí Bartra died; in 1984, Joan Vinyoli; in 1985, Salvador Espriu, and in 1987, J.V. Foix. But there was not a similar generation to replace them, and the younger poets found themselves without immediate models. This coincided with a falling-off of interest in poetry, now that poetry was no longer a weapon nor occupying an ideological position, given that democracy had been established in Spain in 1978, albeit a very weak one.

It is interesting how many women's voices came to the fore at the end of the 1980s, poets who began to be published when they were thirty or forty, such as Teresa Pascual, Montserrat Rodés and Margalida Pons. Pons published two collections while still very young and, for the moment, has not published anything further. The sea and the natural world are present in the poem 'Black Sea' from *Les aus / The Birds*, 1988. The poem is prefaced by a quotation from Lucretius on the Pontus, a sea that always keeps the same regularity in its course. Confronting this, the poetic 'I' questions herself in a profoundly metaphysical way on the imperturbable laws of nature, taking water as an example.

Divided among the four elements is Montserrat Rodés's first book, *La set de l'aigua / Water's thirst*, 1991. Earth's portion is dedicated to the memory of her mother: these are ten short poems in which the poet evokes her mother's death and subsequent memory and desolation. Rodés is a poet of the short line with poems reminiscent of haiku and tanka (incorporated into the Catalan tradition from the beginning of the twentieth century).

Teresa Pascual, likewise a writer of pared-down poems, evokes in *Arena* the solitude, the expressions and places of everyday living, or the search for the loved one. In her poem 'I explore new spaces' the theme of solitude is central, the solitude experienced in an urban landscape full of people, in a strange place which the poet visits, perhaps in order to escape, perhaps to search for the nucleus of her being.

Enric Casasses, born the year before Teresa Pascual, has published fifteen collections since 1992. 'Small Night-scene' is like an ancient romance, with urban landscapes and characters from the late twentieth century, almost an epic poem in which there is a confrontation between the poet (the protagonist) and the police (the forces of oppression). This poem exemplifies Casasses' writing: the sense of irony, the importance of sound, great control over language and meter (idiomatic expressions, onomatopoeia, rhythm, eight-syllable verses with assonantal rhyming).

The young poets of the 1990s lived in a situation completely different from that of the older poets of this anthology. While realising that there is no ideal Catalonia for which to fight, they do not wish to build a new kind of world although they probably do not like their society. Some of them attack earlier poets but fail to elaborate any clear-cut aesthetic. The diversity of their voices might be said to be one of the characteristics of these years, as well as the growth of poetry readings to the detriment of book sales, a fact that gives rise to the importance of the delivery of the poetry by these poets, and the increase in performance poetry, where the poets play with words and sounds, and even with gestures.

Seventeen years younger than Casasses, Forcano published his first two collections in 1993, one of which is *Les mans descalces / Barefoot Hands*. The search for the beloved is the theme of the greater part of this book. In 'Exchange your eyes for mine', external reality is of no importance, given that the poetic 'I' exists only through the beloved. In a sensuous and surrealist image, the poet desires to plunge deep inside the beloved in such a way that words become unnecessary and the only things that matter are the eyes (as explorers of the interior of the other), the hands and the lips (the sense of touch).

'Summer Solstice' is a song to love in its abundance by the Valencian poet M. Josep Escrivà. Using imagery closely related to the natural world and especially to the sea, Escrivà dedicates this poem to Miquel Martí i Pol, a poem of love fulfilled, in which the sense of touch, over the entire skin, acquires great importance, especially in the final verse, where she celebrates love as the source of the poet's words.

Another Valencian, Júlia Zabala, in a highly individual style, denounces the state in which the world, and especially women, now finds itself. Her stanzas recall the verses of the Bible or of the Sufi tradition and, thanks to her use of proper names, suggest an Arab world. They are poems in which war is present, as well as the dead whom war engenders, and the failure of immigrants to adapt to their societies.

Anna Aguilar-Amat, older than the previous poets, published her first book in 2000. In her poems she describes elements and objects of everyday life, which are the pretext for meditating on the passing of time, on love or on death. In her poem 'Insoles', these lead her to reflect on the future of her son, in the hope that he may not repeat his parents' mistakes, but inherit from them something of greater worth.

Twenty-five poems, twenty-five poets, twenty-five ways of scrutinising themselves and of observing the world, a world that is always changing but ever constant, as water is, in which the poet immerses himself or herself, as though in a mirror, in order to discover another reality, intangible but powerful, that shapes our existence.

Many people helped me in producing this anthology, but nothing would have been possible without Anna Crowe. Not only is she one of the translators, but also she helped me in selecting the poems, bringing an invaluable outsider's point of view when we had to choose one poem from among several good ones.

I should also like to thank Carles Torner, Director of Languages and Humanities in the Institut Ramon Llull, and Jaume Subirana, Director of the Institució de les Lletres Catalanes, for their enthusiastic support for the project; the former Director of the Institució de les Lletres Catalanes, Francesc Parcerisas, who first made contact with the Scottish Poetry Library; Glòria Bordons, for her help with the poem by Joan Brossa; and Carles Rebassa, the Mallorcan poet and student of Blai Bonet, for all the help he offered Anna Crowe and myself, in particular in explaining the intricacies of Bonet's poem.

Finally, my thanks go to the poets who appear in the anthology, or their heirs, who were so ready to give their permission for publication, to Robyn Marsack from SPL for her help and support and to Carcanet for making this book possible.

Iolanda Pelegrí
Barcelona, November 2006

THE POEMS

Iris blaus

Quina pell més suau oferiu als abraços de l'aire,
iris blaus.
        Ja l'abril ens ha dut
els terrors de la mort, de la carn masegada, dels ossos
estellats, mentre infants innocents
entre flors parlotegen, treuen brots tan efímers
com els arbres: no ho saben.
Però un vol d'ala rasant, al captard,
els ennuvola els ulls amb bromes de sospita,
un biaix estrident els solca el front puríssim
i ens miren esverats
mentre el vent tan suau de l'abril mou els iris.

Iris blaus que floreixen sobre la terra flonja,
iris blaus dels jardins de les cases dels rics, excessius,
iris blaus camperols dels marges: tots els iris
per l'abril ens consolen amb la seva pell tendra
i ens torben
amb el seu perfum tèrbol d'olor de nen malalt.

1978 | Narcís Comadira

Blue Irises

What soft skin you offer the air's embraces,
blue irises.
                April has already put on for us
the terrors of death, of crushed flesh, splintered
bones, while innocent children
prattle among flowers, they put out shoots as ephemeral
as trees: they do not know this.
But the flight of a wing skimming low towards evening
clouds their eyes with a fog of unease,
a harsh roar as it banks creases their smooth brows
and they gaze at each other in terror
while the oh-so-gentle April breeze ruffles the iris.

Blue irises blossoming over the soft earth,
blue irises, immoderate in the gardens of rich men's houses,
blue irises growing wild along the banks: all the irises
in April console us with their tender skin
and disturb us
with their muddy scent, that smell of a sick child.

translated by Anna Crowe | 1978

Mar brut

Pel cel encapotat, ni un raig de sol.
Et miro cargolant-te, mar
bròfec, estèril,
massa ocupat en tu mateix,
bramant,
         les ones rebolcant-se
sense recurs.
        On trenquen, les gavines
van en rengle pacífic a l'aguait
de les deixalles
que els portes, brut.
        Aquestes coses
em fan senyals, visc estranyant-me'n. Miro,
busco el sentit:
        així faig moure peces,
de casa a casa, en el tauler del temps,
per màgia o per precepte:
        jocs
per ajornar la mort.

1979 | Joan Vinyoli

Grubby Sea

No ray of sun pierces the cloud-filled sky.
Surly, sterile sea, I watch
you coil in excessive
self-preoccupation,
then roar when your waves
                              crash in upon each other
as if imprisoned.
                    Where they break,
seagulls line up peacefully, scavenging
for the flotsam you bring them,
grubby as yourself.
                    All of these
things are signs to me, provoke
a puzzlement that is my life. Watching,
I seek their meaning:
                          as, across time's chessboard,
I move pieces from house to house, casting
spells when I fail to observe the rules,
                                        in games
whose aim is to keep death at bay.

translated by Christopher Whyte | 1979

Paraules per a un lapidari

Perquè Joan Miró troba una pedra.
Perquè Joan Miró
ha collit una pedra. Mireu l'aigua del sol
i aquest gust que té l'herba,
aquest gust de verd d'herba,
aquestes vetes de la pedra verda:
el Verb, tot fet de vetes rocalloses.
Perquè Joan Miró toca les pedres:
n'hi ha una que tan sols és un fil d'aigua arrecerant-se als masos.
Perquè Joan Miró esguarda les pedres:
claror de temple de Baal, claror del mar d'Ur i d'Astarte,
claror de torxa al clos d'Eleusis, claror del tronc de l'olivera.
Perquè Joan Miró escolta les pedres:
campanes de color terrós com l'orpiment,
esquelles primes com la matinada,
batalls de bronze al sot obac de l'herbolari,
campanes d'or en una sala groga
i el crit de les ales dels ànecs al cor d'una nit de tardor.
Totes les veus de la pedrisseria,
totes les llums pedreres,
la pedruscada als vidres, amb un so de fiscorns,
i aquell roc vermellós quan vespreja,
i un pensament d'herbei a les esquerdes fosques,
i la caputxa verda del botànic.
i la gonella del mineralista,
i el remeier que cull pedres al cim del bosc llampeguejant
i, per camins de carro, entoma el xàfec,
i no va moll de pluja,
no és pas moll de pluja,
per la virtut que cada pedra té.
I ara el cel ha tancat el seu castell de cartes, que tant flamarejava,
i al fons de l'armari dels núvols lluu només una pedra:
un present de la fosca i la llum que acaba de collir Joan Miró.

1980 | Pere Gimferrer

Words for a stonecutter

Because Joan Miró comes upon a stone.
Because Joan Miró
has picked one up. Look at the sun's
water and the taste the grass has,
this taste of grassy green,
these ribbons in green stone:
the Word, entirely made of ribbons in rock.
Because Joan Miró is touching the stones:
one is nothing more than a thread of water the farms protect.
Because Joan Miró scrutinises the stones:
translucence of Baal's Temple, of the sea of Ur and Astarte,
of a torch in the precinct at Eleusis, translucence of an olive trunk.
Because Joan Miró is listening to the stones:
bells with the earthen colour of orpiment,
cowbells delicate as breaking day,
bronze clappers in the herbalist's shady den,
bells of gold in a yellow room
and the cry of ducks' wings at the heart of an autumn night.
A symphony of stoniness,
all possible quarry lights,
stones hailing on window panes with a sound like bugles
and that rock, reddening as evening falls,
a hint of undergrowth in gloomy crevices
and the botanist's green hood,
the mineralogist's apron,
the healer gathering stones high in the glittering wood,
following rutted tracks beneath the downpour;
the rain cannot make him wet,
cannot make him wet at all,
because of the virtue intrinsic to each stone.
And now the sky has shut its house of cards whose flames leapt high,
and deep in the cupboard of clouds all that shines is a stone:
a gift from darkness and light Joan Miró just gathered.

translated by Christopher Whyte | 1980

'M'aixecaré del llit'

M'aixecaré del llit
i de l'insomni.
En obrir la porta,
rebré una bafarada
d'aire calent, mentre
els ulls se submergiran
en la frescor d'uns
pins, llunyans. Després,
prendré el càntir del racó,
i l'alçaré entre els meus
braços i sentiré
el doll viu
de l'aigua que refresca
la gola seca de
paraules no dites.

1981 | Montserrat Abelló

'I will get up...'

I will get up from my bed
and from insomnia.
When I open the door,
I will receive a gust
of hot air, while
my eyes will pierce
the coolness of some
pines, far-off. Then,
I'll take the pitcher from its place
and lift it in my
arms and I'll feel
the living stream
of water that refreshes
my throat, dry from
unuttered words.

translated by Anna Crowe | 1981

'Guaita!'

Guaita! Tenim les mans de la mateixa mida!
I les meves per grosses, les teves per menudes!
Veus? L'ocell fosc ha baixat a l'onada
i el peix de llum s'ha ajocat a la branca.

La branca és aigua i l' onada treu fulles.
El peix fosqueja entre el velam de l'aire.
L'ocell és clar. La lluna, submarina.
Guaita! Tenim les mans de la mateixa mida.

L'ona tragina fruita al grat del vent.
La branca trenca als esculls del capvespre.
Lluna de nacre, gavadals de boira
ens capgiren la casa i la tendresa.

Ja ni sabem on s'han trobat, amor,
les nostres mans de la mateixa mida.

1982 | Maria Mercè Marçal

'Look!'

Look! Your hands and mine are the same size!
Though mine are big and yours are tiny!
Do you see? The dark bird has swooped to the wave
and the shining fish has gone to roost on the branch.

The branch is water and the wave puts forth leaves.
The fish grows dark among the sails of the air.
The bird is pale. The moon, underwater.
Look! Your hands and mine are the same size!

The wave carts fruit at the wind's pleasure.
The branch breaks on the reefs of evening.
Mother-of-pearl moon, and mists galore
turn house and tenderness upside-down.

Nor do we know, love, how they found each other,
these hands of ours that are the same size.

translated by Anna Crowe | 1982

Anna dorm

Anna dorm al meu costat.
Jo tinc el flanc lancinat.
Dorm, Anna, ferro i bondat.
Algú, en un moment beat,
va creure el món ben creat.
Anna dorm, castell gebrat.
Saps, Anna, el gall ha cantat,
i no te n'has adonat
des del teu son ancorat.
Anna dorm al meu costat.
Jo tinc el flanc lancinat.
Saps, Anna, el gall ha cantat.

Dorm, Anna meva, dorm, amb la testa mansa
com acatant la nit.
Regina de la pau, que en traüt i bonança
governes amb un dit.

Des del meu desconhort, dic les epifanies:
primer surt del teu front
el nostre solixent, l'astre dels nostres dies:
corona, vol i món.

Surt la lluna després, lluna de nuviatges
que entrà a casa a Roissy
i fou el testimoni dels primers abordatges
dels nus de tu i de mi.

De la teva mà dreta s'aixeca, amor, l'au ígnia
que allunya tots els gels
i se t'enrosca a l'ombra, com si fos una insígnia,
el llarg serpent d'estels.

Non-non, Anna, non-non – dic amb la veu de llana.
El gall canta de nou.
Ning-nong, amor, ning-nang – dic amb veu de campana
tatuada pel rou.

1983 | Agustí Bartra

Anna Sleeps

Anna lies sleeping by my side.
My side has been pierced.
Sleep, Anna, iron and kindness.
Someone, in a blessed time,
thought the world well-made.
Anna lies sleeping, frosty heap.
Anna, you know, the cock has crowed,
but you've not stirred
out of your anchored sleep.
Anna lies sleeping by my side.
My side has been pierced.
Anna, you know, the cock has crowed.

Sleep, my Anna, go on sleeping, head bowed
as though in reverence to the night.
Queen of peace, for in wild or in fine weather
you steer with just one finger.

In my distress, I say the epiphanies:
first there rises from your brow the light
of the rising sun, the star of all our days:
                          corona, world and flight.

Then after comes the moon, of all things bridal
            that entered the house at Roissy
and was a witness of the first grapplings
            of a naked you and me.

From your right hand rises, love, the fire-
            bird that dispels all ice
and coiled about you in the shade, like some device,
            the serpent made of stars.

Hush-a-bye, Anna, hush-a-bye – I say with a voice of wool.
            The cock crows as it must.
Ding-dong, ,my love, ding-dang – I say with the voice of a bell
            that is tattooed with rust.

translated by Anna Crowe | 1983

Non-non, Anna, non-non – dic amb veu de pistil,
ning-nong, Anna, ning-nang – dic, freturós d'asil.

Volia dir amb veu baixa la teva alta lloança
i gairebé destrio el cant que no descansa.
Però t'he dit amor. I és tot, és tot, és tot.
Des de l'esper, pregunto: farem florir el sanglot?

Anna dorm al meu costat.
Jo tinc el flanc lancinat.

Dorm, Anna, ferro i bondat.
Saps, Anna, el gall ha cantat
i alguna cosa ha passat.
Anna, què tens a l'esguard?
Mira, el penell ha girat.

Venen genets de clarors!

El gall canta per tots dos.

Hush-a-bye, Anna, hush-a-bye – I say in the voice of a pistil,
ding-dong, Anna, ding-dang – I say, desperate for shelter.

I wanted to say in a low voice your high praises
and barely discern the song which never wearies.

But I said love to you. And that is everything, everything, everything.
Out of my hope I ask you: shall we make sorrow flower?

Anna lies sleeping by my side.
My side has been pierced.

Sleep, Anna, iron and kindness.
Anna, you know, the cock has crowed
and something else has happened.
Anna, what does that look mean?
See, the weathercock has changed.

Bright riders are arriving!

The cock crows for us both.

translated by Anna Crowe | 1983

Somni

Com llops sanats menjant flors de baladre
els pelegrins s'engaten en luxosos bordells,
en pabs obscurs, entre poemes i anís.
Es regalen carícies fent cops blaus amb sivelles.
Ençaten les malures i llepen tot el pus.
Grogor de galtes tebes, desencís.
Foc de solitud i suc d'herba barata.
Fulles de carxofera, lletrada de cascall,
tabac de picadura.

El renou no és l' excusa de converses cremades
entre bafles vibrants i focus com d'acer.
Els gargalls de l' agrura inunden les moquetes
i cap ocell no hi ha que niui arran dels bars.
Bucs esguerrats als costers de les pletes.
Penyals formigonats que no tasten la mar.
¿Qui triarà les pomes escaldades?

La calç cobreix tots els cossos vençuts.

1984 | Damià Huguet

Dream

Like gelded wolves munching oleander blossoms
pilgrims get pissed in opulent whorehouses,
in shady pubs, surrounded by poems and absinth.
Caresses are bruising blows dealt with their buckles.
They start up plagues by licking all the pus.
Jaundiced, throbbing cheeks and disillusion.
Isolation aflame, quintessence of cheap grass.
Artichoke foliage, crushed poppy juice,
shredded tobacco.

Pandemonium cannot mitigate
conversations consumed by fire amidst
sonic screens shuddering, lenses sharp as steel.
Spluttered bile inundates the moquette
and not one bird is nesting on the bars.
Misshapen dents disfigure the sheepfolds' sides.
Concrete slabs that never taste the sea.
Who will choose from among the bruised figs?

Lime shrouds all the bodies of the defeated.

translated by Christopher Whyte | 1984

Sala egípcia

M'assec a la sala egípcia del museu
i sento el brunzir de mel de les abelles.
El passat és de debò: groc i blau,
com el blat que agrana el pagès o aquesta cigonya
que beu al riu turquesa del papir.
Un cop més tot em sembla igual:
el paleta amb el sedàs a bat de sol
i l'esclau que venta, submís, el faraó
m'esperen dins un taxi, carrer avall.
Un vol d'ànecs rabents creua el cel enterbolit;
a la taula del costat, l'ibis somica, ebri, cruel.
Diuen que les passions no es poden mai pintar
però aquest fresc és un mirall de quatre mil anys.
Vindrà la mort, com el gos fosc de la paret,
i creurem ser massa joves, o immadurs,
o ens sabrà greu de traspassar, adormits,
el goig escàs i fugisser de tants moments perduts.
La barca, però, llisca eterna sota el sol roent.

The Egyptian Room

I sit in the Egyptian room in the museum
and hear the honeyed buzzing of the bees.
The past is with us, now: yellow and blue,
like the wheat the labourer is threshing, or that stork
that drinks from the turquoise river of the papyrus.
Once again all times seem to be one and the same:
the stone-mason with his sieve in the scorching sun,
and the slave who is humbly fanning the pharaoh
wait for me in a taxi down the street.
A flock of ducks swiftly crosses the murky sky;
at the next table the ibis snivels, drunk and tyrannical.
They say the passions can't be painted any longer
but this four-thousand-year-old fresco is a mirror.
Death will come, like that black dog on the wall,
and we'll think ourselves too young, not ripe enough,
or we'll lament our having to fall asleep and leave behind
so many moments' scant and fleeting joy, all lost.
But look at the boat, gliding forever under the blazing sun.

translated by Anna Crowe | 1985

XIV

PREHISTÒRIA DE TOTES LES RECERQUES LA PLATJA VORA L'ALT
PENYA-SEGAT A LA COSTA NORD DE L'ILLA I LA CAIGUDA INCESSANT
DE L'AIGUA DES DEL CAPDAMUNT FINS A LA SORRA EL PERFIL
MIRANT CASCADES DES D'ALLÍ ON ES VA ALÇAR LA FIGURA ESVELTA
QUE PRESIDIA TOTES LES NAIXENCES TOTES LES RECERQUES LA
MIRADA REFLECTINT ELS ASTRES QUE NO HA DESCOBERT NINGÚ

> *Mundo de lo prometido,*
> *agua.*

Aigua de violins malalts de vida,
aigua torrencial del descobrir,
aigua del llac que no serà la mort
sinó allò que hi havia de promesa
dins el corrent. Aigua de l'esperança,
joncs que degoten, canyissars que es gronxen
i allò que ara ens contorba i ens resum
les incerteses, solituds i esperes,
tot amagant finalitats al mot
i sentint, doncs, el misteri de l'aigua
que cau del cingle a pocs passos del mar:
la cascada que ens sap espectadors.
Aquí, de matinada, l'aigua parla
de naixences, d'oblits, de llunyanies
que subratllen els crits de les gavines.
A frec de l'aigua passa la tendresa
com si es mesclés amb llàgrimes que cauen
d'un aire que es va omplint de claredat.
La buscarem en closos que ens atrauen.
La buscarem amb l'anhel que ens amara.

1986 | Feliu Formosa

XIV

PREHISTORY OF ALL QUESTS THE BEACH BY THE HIGH PRECIPICE ON
THE NORTH COAST OF THE ISLAND AND THE CEASELESS FALLING
OF THE WATER FROM THE SUMMIT TO THE SAND THE PROFILE
OBSERVING WATERFALLS FROM THE POINT WHENCE AROSE THE
SLENDER FORM WHICH PRESIDED OVER ALL BIRTHS ALL QUESTS
THE GAZE REFLECTING THE STARS NO-ONE HAS DISCOVERED

> *Mundo de lo prometido,*
> *agua.*

Water of violins diseased with life,
torrential water of discovery,
water of the lake which will not be
death but instead the promise borne along
by the current. Water of hope,
dripping reedbeds, swaying canebrakes
all that disturbs us now, all that embodies
solitudes, uncertainties and waiting,
all that hides the purpose from the word
and therefore feels the water's mystery
dropping off the crag a few steps from the sea:
the waterfall that knows we're watching it.
Here, before daybreak, the water speaks
of birth, forgetfulness, of distant lands
to which the seagulls' cries lend emphasis.
Tenderness passes, skimming the water's surface
as if it could mingle with the tears distilled
from an atmosphere that clarity is filling.
We'll seek it in the recesses that draw us.
We'll seek it with the longing we are drenched in.

translated by Christopher Whyte | 1986

Lo pus bell catalanesc del món

Lentes alzines, maternals figueres,
pollancres cristal·lins, dring de font viva,
esclarissades ombres de l'oliva,
armat esvalot mut de romegueres,
el pomerar pintat, fresques pereres,
arrodonida eufòrbia, pleta freda,
amb flors l'albó com d'engruixada seda,
roques llises, capblaus, esparregueres,
pedra amb un liquen, groc com la moneda
del temps que calla entre les caderneres,

blaus, espigats espígols, llentrisqueres
mates enceses, escanya-rossins,
fua aturada dels cabridencs pins
que s'enfilen amb xiulo a les voreres
d'arran de mar, esmusses carritxeres,
escambuixades penyes, vent gregal,
mar: esperit escènic, fonda sal,
roques brescades, conques salineres...
Ran de rel com llengua romanial
pateix flor el romaní de les caeres.

1987 | Blai Bonet

The most beautiful Catalan in the world

Slow-growing holm-oaks, motherly arms of figs,
clear-cut poplars, the spring's voice welling,
the olive-tree's thin shade fraying,
brambles' silent riot of barbed twigs,
the painted apple-orchard, cool pears,
soft mounds of spurge, the sheep-pen standing cold,
blooms on the asphodel in thick silken folds,
smooth rocks, asparagus-fern, cornflowers,
stone with lichen on it like time's own gold
lying abashed among the goldfinch showers,

blues, spindly lavender, mastic-trees'
blazing leaves, reeds with goading spines,
arrested headlong flight of goatish pines
that clamber downhill in the whistling breeze
to paths beside the sea, to blunted reeds,
dishevelled crags, the wind that blows from Greece,
sea: dramatic genius, salty deeps,
rocks like honeycomb, salt-pan creeks...
Close to the ground, like common speech once more
made whole, the cliff-top rosemary bears flowers.

translated by Anna Crowe | 1987

Mar Negra

«Que l èter, en efecte, pot fluir amb
regularitat i amb un delit uniforme,
ens ho demostra el Pontos, un mar
que s'escola segons un corrent im-
mutable, conservant sempre la ma-
teixa regularitat en el seu curs.»

He tremolat sentint
els corrents que m'envolten,
les aigües somes renovant la sal
de cambres closes,
la claror degotant a poc a poc
als estimballs.
He begut foc, he ofert el meu tresor,
galant, a l'oceà,
he occit els peixos que la nit,
amb inútil somrís, em reclamava.

P'rò a la fondària,
on no se'm du cap força
                          i on la vida
és un record al desert de la pedra,
m'he mantingut clavat amb ulls immòbils,
sols escoltant els polzes insistents
sota el gran cor del mar,
l'obscur batec que amb veu sense ressons
fa estremir-se la terra.

1988 | Margalida Pons

Black Sea

'That the ether can indeed flow regularly
and with unvarying delight
is proven to us by the Euxine Sea, drained by
a constant current whose flow
follows one single, unchanging rhythm.'

My trembling started when I sensed
the currents which surround me,
the shallows where the salt
of enclosed spaces is regenerated,
the clarity distilled drop after drop
upon the precipices.
I have drunk fire, have gallantly offered my treasure to
the ocean, slain those fish the night,
uselessly smiling, demanded of me.

Far, far below, however,
where no force carries me
                                    where life
is but remembered in a stony desert,
I froze rigid, eyes motionless,
merely detecting the unceasing throb
beneath the sea's huge heart,
vague rhythm whose unechoing tones
set the earth a-tremble.

translated by Christopher Whyte | 1988

Trofeu

Per a un amic escultor

El vent pregunta. Al cau mateix del vent,
respon el còdol
enfonyat entre brins de palla i de tenebra.
I mireu-li la galta, llisa, vibràtil,
quan l'alosa s'enfila, canta que canta.

Respon el vent.
Alt i senyor, petja i urpeja.
Amb la capa ocel·lada, damunt l'esbarzerar,
la nit s'avara, doctoralment.
Tan dret i negre, mireu com el nauxer
llisca segur entre els pètals de l'alba.

Res de paisatge. Tot és sabut, premut,
resolt en abraçada musculosa
i abandó de parpelles.

Només, a l'horitzó,
tants i tants horitzons que ens bateguen als polsos,
a la ratlla d'un dia i cada dia,
com a llast, el darrer, del darrer aire,
pesos de fruita i de colors
per a quina justícia o bé tendresa?

Com si,
en marbre i bronze, en gropes i malucs,
s'alzinés ara o mai la caricia del sol,
i un contrapunt obac de notes greus i tinta
enclogués el secret d'alguna alta victòria.

1989 | Jordi Sarsanedas

Trophy

to a sculptor friend

The wind asks. Deep in the wind's lair
a pebble answers,
wedged among wisps of straw and darkness.
Observe its smooth, pulsating cheek as the lark
takes to the skies in uninterrupted song.

The wind answers.
Tall, masterful, treading on claws that tear.
In birdlike cape, above the bramble thicket
night lifts a dogmatic anchor.
So straight, so black, observe the mariner
slip unerringly between dawn's petals.

Absence of a landscape. Everything is known,
compressed, issues in muscular embrace,
abandoning of eyelids.

But, on the skyline,
skyline on skyline throbbing at our wrists,
at a day's edge and every day's
like a dead weight, the last, of the last air,
swags of fruit and colours profiting
what justice or what tenderness?

As though,
marble and bronze, hips and hindquarters,
the sun's caress should now or never draw
itself erect, and a shadowy counterpoint
of deep-toned notes and ink were to embody
the secret of some lofty victory.

translated by Christopher Whyte | 1989

Post-scriptum

Hi ha platges en les planes d'aquest llibre
on començar el mateix amor i, encara,
somriure des dels versos.
Sempre estaràs amb mi si puc escriure.
Tu seràs jo i t'estimaré a les fosques
perquè la corrosiva llum dels dies
reduiria a pols aquestes ones
de la mar que contemplo amb els teus ulls.
Només així ens emparen,
les pròpies paraules, de l'infern
del seu significat, i ens endinsem
en l'edat roja, sempre amb l'horitzó
de l'illa del tresor al nostre front.

1990 | Joan Margarit

Postscript

There are beaches in the pages of this book
where love itself might begin, and where
we might even smile out from the poems.
You will always be with me if I can write.
You will be me and I will love you in the darkness
because the days´ corrosive light
would reduce to dust these waves
of the sea that I gaze at with your eyes.
This is the only way particular words
shelter us from the hell
of their meaning, and we plunge deeper
into red age, with the horizon
of the treasure island always before us.

translated by Anna Crowe | 1990

III

No hem dit res, només l'ofec al pit,
la llum endormiscada sobre els arbres,
el verd esvaït del desig, la set
de l'aigua. —La música desolada
cau per camins encongits de basarda.

IV

Cuso l'abril als teus
ulls—ara de foc, ara
de cendra—amb els fils
rosegats per silencis.

Enfilalls de mi, deixo,
al port blau dels teus anys,
lluny de l'àrida terra
que ens prem i ens esqueixa.

—Sota el sol: un somrís
de plom, un gest amarg
que desfà el meu nom,
entre ones robades.

X

La terra es clou cansada.
Plany de campanes. Dorm
el silenci de cendra
en el buit de les branques.
Esquerp, el vent fereix
la nostra tarda. Fugen
aus amb foc a les ales.

III

We have said nothing, only the tightness in the chest,
the drowsy light above the trees,
the faded green of desire, water´s
thirst. – Desolate music
falls on shrunken paths of fear.

IV

I sew April into your
eyes – now fire, now
ash – with threads
gnawed by silence.

Strings of myself I leave
in the blue port of your years
far from the arid land
that presses and shreds us.

– Under the sun: a leaden
smile, a sour expression
that undoes my name,
among stolen waves.

X

Earth wearily closes.
Lament of bells. Ash's
silence sleeps
in the branches´ emptiness.
The wind is harsh and wounds
our afternoon. Birds
flee with wings on fire.

translated by Anna Crowe | 1991

'Camine nous espais'

Camine nous espais *Unter den Linden*
amb la por de qui pensa a escapar
i es troba ja perdut des de l'inici.
Explore una defensa entre les cares
que marxen sense veu i sense nom
dins d'un metro tancat com una asfíxia
i encalle en gels de blanca solitud
mentre avança el desert del soterrani.
I per què ara no puc *Unter den Linden*
notar la pau i l'ombra dels til·lers
si res no tinc, si ja no tinc de mi
més que el meu vell, el meu trist testimoni.

1992 | Teresa Pascual

'I explore new spaces'

Unter den Linden I explore new spaces
with the fear of one who meditates
escape yet gets lost at the very start,
interrogate a possible defence
among voiceless, nameless faces marching
within the metro's suffocating closeness,
run aground in ice-white loneliness
while the desert underworld proceeds
given that right now, *Unter den Linden*,
the lime-trees' peace and their shade are as nothing
since I am dispossessed, and of myself
have only the old, sad witness I bear.

translated by Christopher Whyte | 1992

'Dóna'm els teus ulls'

Dóna'm els teus ulls
i pren els meus.
Així, quan ploris,
em rectificaràs la sang
de sal, i veuràs també quins pous més fons
s'obren en mi quan sembla que ric
o cantussejo.
Dóna'm els teus ulls
i pren els meus.
Així podré veure com se't fan els mots a dins
abans de ser la teva veu.
I no caldrà parlar, no caldrà el dolor.

I no et preocupis:
amb les mans ens buscarem els llavis
a l'hora de besar-nos.

1993 | Manuel Forcano

'Exchange your eyes for mine'

Exchange your eyes for mine.
In crying, you can set
my blood's salt content right,
and learn how deep the wells that open in me are
when all I seem to do is laugh
or hum a tune.
Exchange your eyes for mine.
Then I can learn the inner making of your words
before you utter them.
Talk will be superfluous, and pain.

Don't worry:
our hands will trace our lips
at the moment of each kiss.

translated by Christopher Whyte | 1993

Petita escena nocturna

En una cantonada pobra
d'un carrer vell un bar nocturn
de tant en tant obre la porta
i n'ix la música i el fum.

Hi ha quatre motos aparcades,
les fulles dormen als balcons,
a les parets escrostonades
cares pintades i oracions.

Passen altius sis policies
creient que són un grup de rock
en busca de verges, de víctimes
pel seu altar d'armes de foc

i t'acorralen entre els cotxos
i la paret i escorcollant
no et troben res ni fins al forro:
només tens l'ànima il·legal.

A crits et diuen que te'n vagis
i se'n van ells, són collonuts,
perdonavides, trinitaris,
sabent que no t'han conegut.

En una cantonada estreta
torna la calma i el xiu-xiu,
una persiana verda peta
i al portal un, begut, fa el riu.

1994 | Enric Casasses

Small Night-scene

From time to time, on a poor corner
of an old street, the swinging door
of an all-night bar pours out
smoke and music into the air.

Outside, four mopeds are left parked,
leaves sleep on the balconies,
the dilapidated walls are marked
with painted faces, litanies.

Six arrogant police pass by
acting as though they were rock stars, big guns
cruising for virgins or some poor guy
to leave on their altar of heaped-up weapons

and they pin you between the cars and the wall
and investigate you down to the folds
of your blameless vest, but the only illegal
thing you're carrying is your soul.

They yell at you and tell you to beat it
then leave themselves, they're a waste of space,
hectoring bullies, failed jesuits,
knowing they didn't know your face.

On a corner of two narrow streets
peace returns, and the usual whispers,
while a green window-shutter creaks
and in the doorway a drunk pisses.

Translated by Anna Crowe | 1994

Sonet sense retoc

No van vestits de seda tots els arbres
ni en sap tothom de treballar la terra.
A la ciutat no planten gaires arbres
i si t' enfiles gaire caus a terra.

Han empedrat la Ment sota alguns arbres
i cau la neu sobre el planeta Terra.
El món és un boscatge de pocs arbres
i no han fet cap pacte mar i terra.

Cada cosa refà ben poca feina;
em sento nàufrag entremig de festes
i la paraula em dóna molta feina.

Sé les voltes que fan feines i festes.
Aixeco la bandera de la feina
i no penso parar fins passat festes.

A Pepa

1995 | Joan Brossa

Plain Sonnet

Not all of them go dressed in silk, our trees,
nor do we all know how to work the earth.
In cities it is seldom they plant trees,
and climb too high, you´re bound to fall to earth.

They´ve paved over the Mind beneath some trees,
and snow is falling on to planet Earth.
The world´s a wood in which there are few trees
and they have signed no treaty, sea and earth.

Few things can be restored through any work;
I´m like a shipwrecked man amid the feasting
and words are what I reap from my hard work.

I know how they change places, work and feasting.
I´m hoisting in the air the banner work
and shan't desist until they´ve done with feasting.

for Pepa

translated by Anna Crowe | 1995

L'àngel de la mort

En la perdurable carència
de la llum

d'os i turquesa és el blau
de la vena:
                la meva veu
plana sobre la teva veu.

Només així s'endinsa l'alba
dins el suburbi cruel que habita
l' ombra,
                la sang, el metall fred,
llengua per la font de mercuri
consumida.

Aleteig sobre la neu quallada.

Un dia més, a cau d' orella,
suborno l'àngel de la mort.

The Angel of Death

In the enduring absence
of light

the blue of the vein is bone
and turquoise:
                    my voice
hovers above your voice.

This is the only way dawn
penetrates the cruel suburb where
the shadow dwells,
                        blood, cold metal,
tongue consumed in the flow
of mercury.

Wing-beats over the curdled snow.

One more day, I whisper,
bribing the angel of death.

translated by Anna Crowe | 1996

Punt i final

Ho deixo tot, però estreno claror.
Faré un pas més i fugiré de mi
per preservar l'empremta d'un desig
que sé que mai no m'abandonarà.
Perdre la hisenda em dóna llibertat.
El mirall s'ha trencat en mil bocins
i en cadascun m'hi veig, desmesurat.
Amor, amor que em crides quan no hi sóc,
¿per quins camins massa sovint te'm perds
si et duc al sexe, al cor i al pensament?
Ho deixo tot i aprenc codis secrets
en el silenci lúcid de la nit.
Demà em dibuixaré en una paret,
demà passat, si em vaga, faré el mort
i al tercer dia ressuscitaré.
Després els versos es riuran de mi
i jo em riuré dels versos, complagut.
Seré molts o potser no seré cap.
Ho deixo tot, aprofiteu-se'n, gent.
Al que no sóc li agrada el desgavell.
Tot el turment em turmenta ben poc.
Només un cos de dona em fa feliç
i ara el descric tancant, solemne, els ulls.
Espero el llamp que m'ha de redimir.
A poc a poc, em posaré dempeus.
S'apropa el gran moment. Ho deixo tot.

1997 | Miquel Martí i Pol

Full stop and Close

I leave it all, yet can broach clarity.
One more step and I shall escape myself
in order to hold fast to the imprint
of a desire I know will not forsake me.
Losing the estate brings me liberty.
The mirror shatters to a thousand fragments
each of them reflecting a huge me.
Oh love that summons me when I am absent
what paths lead you all too often astray
if I carry you in my sex, my heart, my thought?
I leave it all, discover secret codes
within the lucid silence of the night.
I'll draw myself tomorrow on a wall,
the next day, if I feel like it, I'll act
dead, and rise again on the third day.
After that verses will laugh at me
and I shall laugh at them, self-satisfied.
I may be many, or not even one.
I leave it all, get from it what you can.
The me I am not takes delight in chaos.
All of the torment fails to torment me.
Only a woman's body makes me happy:
now I describe it, eyes closed, solemnly
and wait for the redemptive thunderbolt.
Little by little I'll get to my feet.
The great day draws near and I leave it all.

translated by Christopher Whyte | 1997

Solstici d'estiu

...Totes
les claredats acaben en sorpresa.
Miquel Martí i Pol

Has davallat del sol per solcs de teules brunes,
com l'escuma a la pell de molsa de les roques,
com la mar a les mans escasses d'un infant.

Els astres atiaven afalacs de gesmil,
quan només la foscor anunciava a les palpes
dos cossos desbordats en carícies mudes.

Ara que sé el secret, m'esfullaré la pell
de papallones velles i em perdré en el miracle
d'un cos equivocat. I el teu nom fet de vidre
serà causa precisa de les meues paraules.

1998 | M. Josep Escrivà

Summer Solstice

All
clarities climax in a surprise.
Miquel Martí i Pol

You arrived from the sun down furrows of brown tiles,
like foam along the seaweed skin of rocks,
like seawater in a child's tiny hands.

The stars revived blandishments of jasmine
as only groping in the dark proclaimed
two bodies breaking bounds in mute caress.

I know the secret now, and will shed
old butterflies from my skin, losing myself
in the miracle of a mistaken body.
Turned to glass, your name will be
the unequivocal prompter of my words.

translated by Christopher Whyte | 1998

Un poeta

UN POETA ÉS COM TOTHOM:
       sent enveja, té cistitis,
       diu mentides, és covard.
       Allò que el diferencia
       —I això ho canvia tot—
       és que té molta memòria.
       És això que li permet
       d' establir molts més contactes.

UN POETA NO FA COSES
       curioses per cridar
       l'interès de les madones.
       Un poeta no fa res:
       parla amb ell i ja fa massa.

UN POETA NO TÉ PARES:
       no n'hauria de tenir:
       és del tot innecessari.

1999 | Miquel Bauçà

A Poet

A POET'S NO DIFFERENT FROM ANYONE ELSE:
      gets jealous, gets cystitis,
      tells lies, is cowardly.
      What sets him apart
      – and this is fundamental –
      is a good memory,
      which gives him the chance
      to set up many more links.

A POET DOESN'T DO
      stupid things to get
      the fair sex's attention.
      He does nothing at all:
      talking to himself is quite enough.

A POET HAS NO PARENTS:
      and shouldn't have:
      there's simply no need.

translated by Christopher Whyte | 1999

'El teu nom gravat'

Tornaré a l' ombra dels teus ulls
Mahmud Darwix

El teu nom gravat en cada fulla d'herba-sana.
De sobte no sé res de tu.
De sobte només recorde que tu em vas servir l'últim te.
El meu nom gravat en cada fulla d'herba-sana.
Vaig ser agraciada amb l'ombra de la teua parra.
Vaig ser beneïda entre totes les dones.
Vaig ser plena de seny i, penedida,
plena de glòria i plomes de gavina.
De sobte només recorde que em feien mal els peus abans de córrer
                    sense documents per una ciutat que no és la meua.
Gràcies per l'aigua i per l'ombra.
Santificat siga el teu nom
enredat entre els meus cabells desesperats.
Ací no em vol ningú, enyore les palmeres, les palmeres, sobretot,
   aquella tendresa d'hores que relliscaven per la teua esquena al meu
                                                compàs.
I no entendre el recel i aquesta ratlla de guix
pintada en terra. I no saber on ets, ni si et tornaré a veure,
ni en quina altra vida ens vam conèixer
i em vas oferir aigua i pau.
No moriré a l'ombra de casa teua.

'Your name engraved...'

I will return to the shade of your eyes
Mahmoud Darwish

Your name engraved on every mint-leaf.
Suddenly I know nothing about you.
Suddenly I remember only that you poured my final glass of tea.
My name engraved on every mint-leaf.
I was reprieved by the shade of your vine.
I was blessèd among all women.
I was filled with understanding and, repentant,
full of glory and seagulls' wings.
Suddenly I remember only that my feet hurt before running with no
                                        papers in a city that isn't mine.
Thank you for the water and the shade.
May your name be blessed
caught in the midst of my despairing hair.
Here no one wants me, I yearn for the palm-trees, for palm-trees
more than anything,
the tenderness of the hours slipping down your back to my rhythm.

And not understanding the mistrust and the line
chalked on the ground. And not knowing where you are or whether
                                        I'll see you again,
or in what other life we knew each other
and you offered me water and peace.
I shall not die in the shade of your house.

translated by Anna Crowe | 2000

'Era dia de mercat'

Era dia de mercat. Els infants jugaven a guerra. Les dones
triaven les verdures, els ous, l'aviram, les patates. El repertori
era una mica limitat, perquè era temps de guerra. Era dia de mercat.

Dos quarts de cinc de la tarda. Els infants jugaven a guerra
quan de sobte, del cel, d'on vénen, diuen, els àngels i els
ocells, queia un xàfec de foc, el cel era l'infern, l'ordre s'havia capgirat.

Tres hores com una eternitat i aquell joc s'extingia. Els
infants ja no jugaven a guerra: la guerra els havia exterminat.
Ara tothom pensava igual, perquè tots els cadàvers pensen el
mateix. I així començava la gran uniformitat.

Mil sis-cents cinquanta-quatre morts i vuit-cents vuitanta-
nou ferits. Quina gesta, senyors, quina gesta! Que el món
prengui model, ja sap el que l'espera. ¿No habitaven als
Andes, els còndors? Per que trien aquestes contrades?
I l'arbre allí, al bell mig, també nafrat, però dempeus.
—I encara no ressuscitat!

'It was market-day'

It was market-day. The little ones were playing at soldiers. The
women were picking out greens, eggs, poultry, potatoes. The choice
was a bit limited, because it was wartime. It was market-day.

Half-past four in the afternoon. The little ones were playing at
soldiers when suddenly, out of the heavens, where angels and birds
come from, so they say, there fell a great rain of fire, heaven was hell,
the natural order was overturned.

Three hours like an eternity and that game was ending. The little
ones no longer played at soldiers, at wars: war had wiped them out.
Now, everyone thought the same, because all corpses think the
same. And so the great uniformity began.

One thousand six hundred and fifty-four dead and eight hundred
and eighty-nine wounded. What an epic achievement, gentlemen,
what an epic achievement! Should the world wish to take this as a
model, it knows what to expect. Don't condors live in the Andes?
Why do they choose these parts? And the tree there, in the midst of
it all, wounded as well, but standing. – And still it does not revive.

translated by Anna Crowe | 2001

Plantilles

Aquestes ja t'han quedat petites. Hi
passo els dits i toco la planta dels
teus peus, el negatiu d'un temps en
què sempre érem junts i els dies que
viuràs quan jo desaparegui. Un futur
que modela l'ortopèdia; la gravetat
que t'ha fet caminar estrany als meus
passos. Trepitja els meus fracassos
com si fossin graons d'una sapiència
antiga, perquè són el bagul que sempre
podràs vendre al traginer que passi.
Digues que la clau l'has perduda, que
et paguin pel seu pes; si troben que és
lleuger dius que són mapes i si el troben
pesant que són gemmes precioses. I després
ves-te'n lluny, camina fins als cims. Regala
una moneda de perdó. Tot el que donis
et durà més lluny.

2002 | Anna Aguilar-Amat

Insoles

These are already too small for you now. I slip
my fingers in and feel the soles
of your feet, the negative both of a time in which
we were always together and also of the days you
will live through when I disappear. A future
modelled for us by orthopaedics, the heaviness
that's made you walk as a stranger to my
footsteps. Tread my failures underfoot
as though they were steps of an ancient
wisdom, because they are the cabin-trunk you can
always sell to a passing carrier.
Tell him you've lost the key, that
they can pay you according to the weight; if they think
that it's too light, say there are maps inside; if they think
it's heavy, precious stones. And afterwards
travel as far as you can, climb right up to the summits. Drop
a coin or two in the forgiveness box. Every bit you give
will carry you that much further.

translated by Anna Crowe | 2002

Biographies and Acknowledgements

The Editors

Volume Editor

IOLANDA PELEGRÍ

Iolanda Pelegrí was born in Barcelona. She obtained a degree in Catalan Philology, after which she completed post-graduate studies in literary translation from English. Since 1990, she has been working at the Institució de les Lletres Catalanes, where she has organised and co-ordinated activities promoting Catalan literature. She has been active in fostering relations between Catalan writers and those working in other languages, in particular through the guest writer programme and poetry translating seminars that are held in the Pyrenean village of Farrera de Pallars. She is now Head of Projects at the ILC. She has prepared works of Catalan writers (Carner, Ors, Plana, and Anna Murià) for publication, and also the poems translated at the first and second Farrera de Pallars seminars.

Series Editor

ROBYN MARSACK

Robyn Marsack was born and grew up in Wellington, New Zealand. She obtained her BA from Victoria University, and a B.Phil. and D.Phil. from Oxford University. She was an editor for Carcanet Press 1982-1987, before moving to Scotland and working as a freelance editor, translator from French, and critic, reviewing poetry regularly for Scottish newspapers. In 2000 she was appointed Director of the Scottish Poetry Library in Edinburgh. She lives in Glasgow. Her published work includes studies of the poetry of Louis MacNeice and Sylvia Plath, and translations of two books by Nicolas Bouvier, *The Scorpion-Fish* (Carcanet, 1987) and *The Way of the World* (Polygon, 1992; Eland, 2007). She co-edited with Ken Cockburn *Intimate Expanses: XXV Scottish poems 1978-2002* (Scottish Poetry Library/Carcanet, 2004).

Poets' Biographies

with sources for the poems

Montserrat Abelló, 1918–

Poet and translator of English. In 1939 she went into exile with her father and, after living in London for a year, she settled in Chile. In 1963, three years after her return to Catalonia, she had her first book published, but it was in the 1990s that her poetic output intensified. Hers is a lean poetry, stripped to the essentials, that searches for meaning *Al cor de les paraules/ At the heart of the words*, the title of her selected poems. She has translated, among others, the work of Plath, Sexton and Rich. She has been translated into various languages, including English and Castilian.

'M'aixecaré del llit', in *Vida diària: Paraules no dites* (Barcelona: La Sal, 1981). Also published in *Al cor de les paraules: obra poètica 1963-2002* (Barcelona: Proa, 2002).

Anna Aguilar-Amat, 1962–

A poet with a doctorate in computing and linguistics, she teaches at the Universitat Autònoma de Barcelona. Her emergence as a poet has been late but meteoric, for her collections *Trànsit entre dos vols/Transit between two flights, Mùsica i escorbut/ Music and scurvy* and *Petrolier/Oil-tanker* have been awarded three of the most prestigious poetry prizes in Catalan literature. In her work she reflects on the meaning and importance of words, her relationship with everyday life and also on the passing of time. She has been translated into Castilian, English and Macedonian, among others.

'Plantilles', in *Mùsica i escorbut* (Barcelona: Edicions 62. Empúries, 2002).

Agustí Bartra, 1908–1982

Poet, playwright and prose writer, he was among those writers who had to go into exile after General Franco came to power. After living in France for a year, he settled in Mexico for almost thirty years, where he continued to write and publish in Catalan – *L'arbre de foc/The fire-bird* and *Quetzalcoatl*, among other volumes. When he returned to Catalonia he took part in various public events and continued to publish poetry: *Poemes del retorn/Homecoming poems, Haikus d'Arinsal/Haikus from Arinsal*. His poetry is rooted in the romantic tradition, vital and humane. He has been translated into many languages, including English, Castilian and Portuguese.

'Anna dorm', in *Obra poètica completa 1979-1982* (Barcelona: Edicions 62, 1983). Also published in *Alguna cosa ha passat: una tria de poesia transparent* (Argentina: L'Aixernador Edicions, 1995).

MIQUEL BAUÇÀ, 1940–2005

Poet and prose writer, born in Felanitx, a village in Mallorca, he settled in Barcelona in 1961. Profoundly affected by the death of his mother when he was twelve, and by his years as a boarder in a religious college, his work reveals a critical, fierce and lucid vision of human existence. Exploring form, his work embraces poems in heptameter *El noble joc/The noble game* and poetic prose ordered in dictionary style *El canvi/The change, El crepuscle encén estels/Twilight kindles the stars, Els estats de convivència/States of connivance, Els somnis/Dreams*. He has been translated into English and Castilian among other languages.

'Un poeta', in *El pou de les lletres* no. M/13-14/N (spring-summer 1999). Also published in *Els estats de convivència* (Barcelona: Empúries, 2001).

BLAI BONET, 1926–1997

Poet, novelist and art critic, born in Santanyí, a village in Mallorca. He studied in the seminary in Palma from 1939 to 1947 when, ill with tuberculosis, he was sent to a sanatorium, an experience reflected in his novel *El mar* (made into a film by Agustí Villalonga). In 1955 he moved to Barcelona, where he worked in publishing and got to know the literary scene. He went back to Mallorca in 1964 and published, among other books, *El poder i la verdor/Power and greenness, El jove/The young man, Nova York/New York, Sonets/Sonnets*. A restless writer, rebellious and nonconformist, he has been translated into various languages, including Castilian, French, Hungarian, Romanian and Russian.

'Lo pus bell catalanesc del món', in *El jove* (Barcelona: Empúries, 1987).

JOAN BROSSA, 1919–1998

Essentially a poet, friend of Joan Miró and Antoni Tàpies, Brossa published with the latter various books, including *Oda a Macià i oda al President Companys/Ode to Macià and ode to President Companys, El Rei de la màgia/ The King of Magic, Carrer de Wagner/Wagner Street*. Poet of the avant-garde, involved with reality, Brossa's work embraces both a wide and diverse subject-matter, and explores a variety of metrical forms that lead him from the cultivation of sonnets and sestinas to visual poetry and poem-objects. His extensive work, more than a hundred and forty published volumes, has been collected in various books, including *Antologia Poètica/ Poetry anthology, Poemes escollits/Selected poems, A partir del silence/Going from silence* and *Memòria encesa/Memory on fire*, this latter selection made by himself. He has been translated into English, French, Portuguese, Swedish.

'Sonet sense retoc', in *Passat festes* (Barcelona: Empúries, 1995).

ENRIC CASASSES, 1951–

Poet, playwright and translator, who has lived in England and Germany. Although his first book appeared in 1972, it was in the 1990s that he began to be published on a regular basis. With a great command of language, he explores new poetic forms, drawing on diverse influences such as mediaeval poetry, baroque, pop and rock. He has formed a school among younger poets, influenced by his literary style and his manner of reciting his work. Several works stand out: *La cosa aquella/That thing, No hi érem/We were not there, Calç/Lime, D'equivocar-se així/On being wrong like this, Plaça Raspall/Raspall Square*. The translator of Blake and Nerval, he has been translated into various languages, including English, Castilian, Italian and Romanian.

'Petita escena nocturna', in *Començament dels començaments i ocasió de les ocasions* (Barcelona: Empúries, 1994).

NARCÍS COMADIRA, 1942–

Born in Girona, Comadira studied Classics and Philosophy in the Seminary of Girona and at the monastery of Montserrat. He began architectural studies and graduated in History of Art. Poet, painter, and translator of poetry (including Auden, Leopardi, Molière), he is also a literary journalist. From 1971 to 1973 he lived in London, studying and acquiring a profound understanding of English literature and, as the fruit of this experience, published *Un passeig pels bulevards ardents/Walk along burning avenues*. With a great command of form he investigates, with irony, the search for happiness, the relationship between art, death and the passing of time. He has been awarded the most important prizes for Catalan literature and has been translated into English, French, Castilian, Italian and Portuguese.

'Iris blaus', in *Terra natal* (Barcelona: La Gaia Ciència, 1978). Published also in *Formes de l'ombra: poesia 1966-2002* (Barcelona: Edicions 62. Empúries, 2002).

MARIA JOSEP ESCRIVÀ, 1968–

A graduate in Spanish philology from the University of Valencia, she works as a teacher and publisher's editor and proof-reader, contributing to reviews and critical studies in literary magazines, and in organising cultural events. 1993 saw the publication of her first collection of poetry, *Remor alè/Murmuring breath*, followed by two further collections, *A les palpentes del vidre/Groping for the window* and *Tots els noms de la pena/All the names for sorrow*. Hers are brief, subtle poems with simple, striking images that explore love, oblivion and the meaning of poetry and words.

'Solstici d'estiu', in *A les palpentes del vidre* (Barcelona: Columna, 1998).

MANUEL FORCANO, 1968–

Doctor in Semitic Philology and translator from Hebrew, Manuel Forcano has taught at the University of Barcelona. Since the publication of his first book in 1992, he has published six books of poems, all of which have won awards. His most recent poetry collections are *Com un persa/Like a Persian* and *El tren de Bagdad/The train from Baghdad*. Translator of English, French, Italian, Hebrew and Arabic, he has translated the poetry of Yehuda Amichai and *The travels of Ibn Batuta*. His poetry is autobiographical (travel, love, memory) with numerous references to the classical world. His work has been translated into Castilian.

'Dona'm els teus ulls', in *Les mans descalces* (Barcelona: Columna, 1993).

FELIU FORMOSA, 1934–

With a degree in German philology, he is a poet, translator and theatre director. He lived in Germany from 1959 to 1960. On his return he took an active part in Catalan theatre groups who fought to have the works of Catalan and foreign writers re-instated in the life of the theatre, especially engaged writers such as Brecht. His poetry, apart from references to his own tradition, clearly looks to Germany for inspiration. Part of his work has been collected in *Darrere el vidre: Poesia 1979-2000/Behind the glass: Poems 1979-2000*. He has translated Brecht, Trakl, Weiss and Villon. He has been translated into Castilian, English and French.

'XIV', in *Semblança* (Barcelona: Edicions del Mall, 1986). Also in *Darrere el vidre Poesia 1979-2000* (Barcelona: Edicions 62. Empúries, 2004).

PERE GIMFERRER, 1945–

Poet, translator, prose writer and literary critic, as well as art and cinema critic, he has written essays on Joan Miró, Antoni Tàpies and Max Ernst. At the age of eighteen he published his first book of poems in Castilian and occupied a prominent position in the new Spanish poetry. With *Els miralls/ The mirrors*, 1970, he continued his poetic output in Catalan, exploring the literary tradition, especially the baroque and avant-garde. His work has been collected in *Obra Catalana completa, I: Poesia*. The translator into Castilian of Catalan poets such as Espriu and Foix, he has been translated into other languages—Castilian, Danish, Italian, Swedish and English.

'Paraules per a un lapidari', in *Els Marges* no. 20 (September 1980). Published also in *El Vendaval* (Edicio 62, 1988) and in *Antologia Poètica* (Barcelona: Edicions 62, 1999).

DAMIÀ HUGUET, 1946–1996

Born in Campos, a town in Mallorca, where he lived all his life, Huguet's interests were poetry, the plastic arts, and cinema. In 1957 he founded a poetry press in order to publish works that didn't get on to the commercial circuits. A cinema critic, the influence of certain techniques of this art is discernible in his work. The author of sixteen poetry collections that reveal his powerful voice, full of musicality and strength, part of his work has been collected in a poetry anthology and made into a musical drama, *Esquena de ganivet/Back of the knife*.

'Somni', in *Els calls del manobre* (Campos: Guaret, 1984). Also published in *Antologia Poètica* (Barcelona: Proa, 1999).

MARIA MERCÉ MARÇAL, 1952–1998

Poet, novelist and essayist, as a child she lived in a little village in the Pla d'Urgell (an area in the province of Lleida). She went to secondary school in Lleida and studied Catalan Philology in the University of Barcelona, where she formed part of a group of Catalan writers and activists who campaigned against the Franco regime, and later took part in feminist movements. From her first collection of poems in 1977, she displayed great mastery of the language and a fresh vision of the condition of women. She translated Colette, Yourcenar and Leonor Fini. She has been translated into other languages, notably English and German.

'Il', in *Sal Oberta* (Barcelona: Llibres del Mall, 1982). Also published in *Llengua abolida* (1973-1988) (Valencia: Eliseu Clement Editor, 1989).

JOAN MARGARIT, 1938–

Poet and architect. He lectured in the School of Architecture in Barcelona. He wrote his first four books in the 1960s and 1970s in Castilian. In 1981 he published his first work in Catalan and by 2005 there were nineteen collections, which he has gathered into two volumes: *Els primers freds: Poesia 1975-1995/The first frosts: Poems 1975-1995* and *Poesia amorosa completa, 1980-2000/Complete love poetry, 1980-2000* (both published by Edicions Proa). Translator of the work of Ferrater and Martí i Pol into Castilian, he has also consistently translated his own work into Castilian. A substantial selection of his work has been translated into English by Anna Crowe (*Tugs in the fog*, Bloodaxe, 2006).

'Post-scriptum', in *Edat Roja* (Barcelona: Columna, 1990). Also published in *Els primers freds: Poesia 1975-1995* (Barcelona: Proa, 2004).

MIQUEL MARTÍ I POL, 1929–2003

Born into a modest family in Osona, an inner region of Catalonia, Martí i Pol was a factory manager until multiple sclerosis rendered him housebound. The author of many works, Martí i Pol became one of Catalonia's most loved poets and the most widely read. From poetry that focused on social issues he went on to write more intimate work, and his main concerns are love, death and the passing of time. Outstanding works of his are *La fàbrica/The factory, Estimada Marta/Dear Martha, Amb vidres a la sang/With glasses in my veins, Llibre d'absències/Book of absences*, and *Llibre de les solituds/Book of solitudes*. He has been translated into many languages, including English, Asturian, Castilian, French, Italian and Romanian.

'Punt i final', in *Llibre de les solituds* (Barcelona: Edicions 62. Empúries, 1997).

JOSEP PALAU I FABRE, 1917–

Poet, dramatist, prose writer, and essayist with an abiding interest in painting, Palau i Fabre studied literature at the beginning of the 1940s and ran the clandestine magazine, *Poesia* (1944-45). In 1945 he went to Paris where he got to know Picasso and Artaud. The author of a not very extensive but deeply worked body of writing, Palau i Fabre has created his own universe in which the poet as alchemist is an essential figure. Outstanding works of his are *Lorca-Picasso, L'extraordinària vida de Picasso/ The extraordinary life of Picasso, Poemes de l'alquimista/The alchemist's poems* and *Les veus del ventríloc/The ventriloquist's voices*. The translator of Rimbaud and Artaud, he himself has been translated into German, English, Castilian, Italian, Dutch and Swedish.

'Era dia de mercat', in *Les veus del ventríloc: Poesia de teatre* (Barcelona: Proa, 2001). First published as a recitative in his work for theatre, *Homenatge a Picasso*.

Francesc Parcerisas, 1944–

Poet, critic, professor of translation at the Universitat Autònoma de Barcelona, he has taught Spanish at Bristol University and was Director of the Institució de les Lletres Catalanes. Since his first book, published in 1967, his work has evolved from poetry of social comment to poetry of experience: daily life understood as a reflection of the eternal themes (love, the passing of time, death). *Triomf del present: Obra poètica (1965-1983/Triumph of the now: Poetic works (1965-1983)* gathers together work published up until that date, and he has subsequently published three books: *Focs d'octubre/October fires, Natura morta amb nens/Still life with children* and *Dos dies més de sud/Two more days south*. The translator of Heaney, Eliot, Pound, Tolkien, he has been translated into English, Castilian, Hebrew, Slovenian, Dutch, Italian, French, Rumanian and Russian.

'Sala egípcia', in *Reduccions*, no. 27 (November 1985). Also published in *Focs d'octubre* (Barcelona: Columna, 1990).

Teresa Pascual, 1952–

Poet and lecturer in philosophy at the Institut de Gandia, she studied philosophy and letters at the University of Valencia. In 1988 she published her first book of poetry, and four more have followed, three of which – *Flexo, Les hores/The hours, El temps en ordre/Time in order* – have received important awards. Hers is an intimate voice that creates atmosphere and emotions with bare, lyric forms. She has translated Hans Magnus Enzenberger's *Sinking of the Titanic*, and the *Complete Poetical Works* of Ingeborg Bachmann.

'Camine nous espais', in *Arena* (Valencia: IVEI Alfons el Magnànim, 2002).

Margalida Pons, 1966–

A poet with an abiding interest in Mallorcan writers, she teaches at the University of Palma de Mallorca where she studied Catalan philology. She received her doctorate from the University of Barcelona and has studied comparative literature at the University of Indiana. The author of only two collections, *Sis bronzes grisos d'alba/Six bronzes grey with dawn* (1986) and *Les aus/The birds* (1988), her poetry reveals a writer of great lyric sensitivity who explores memory, love and desire. She has been translated into English, Castilian and Russian.

'Mar Negra', in *Les aus* (Barcelona: Edicions 62, 1988).

JAUME PONT, 1947–

Poet, critic and university lecturer. He has taught literature at the universities of Poitiers, Naples and Illinois, and at present teaches at the university of Lleida. His poetry, which he began publishing in 1976, reveals an original writer who has been influenced by the French *maudits*, by surrealism and by the Spanish baroque poets. Poet of contrasts and symbols, some of which are reminiscent of the Arab tradition, he searches for the ultimate reality of the human. His work was collected in 1990 in the book, *Raó d'atzar/Hazard's justice*, and recently he published *Vol de cendres/ Flight of ashes* and *Llibre de la frontera/Book of the frontier*. He has been translated into Castilian, Italian and French, among other languages.

'L'àngel de la mort', in *Vol de cendres* (Barcelona: Edicions 62. Empúries, 1996).

MONTSERRAT RODÉS, 1951–

A poet, she works in publishing as an editor. In the 1970s, she began publishing her poems in various magazines; in 1991, after two years' silence, she published her first book of poems, then six further collections, among them, *La set de l'aigua/Water's thirst, Interlínia/Space between two lines, Deleatur/Delete*, and *Immunitat/Immunity*. Her work is reminiscent of haiku or tanka in structure and lyric intensity. She has been translated into English, Russian and Castilian.

'III, IV, X', in *La set de l'aigua* (Barcelona: Edicions 62, 1991).

JORDI SARSANEDAS, 1924–2006

Poet, prose writer, and translator. He studied in France, lectured at the University of Glasgow, lived in Milan, was a teacher at the French Institute in Barcelona, founder of the Agrupació Dramàtica de Barcelona and an editor of literary magazines. The appearance in 1954, of *Mites/Myths*, a collection of stories, introduced something new into fiction of the day through the book's dream-like and surreal atmosphere. This atmosphere makes itself felt in his collected poetry, *Fins a un cert punt: Poesia (1945-1989)/Up to a certain point: Poems (1945-1989)*. More recently he has published, among other books, *Cor meu, el món/My heart, the world*, *Com una tornada, sí,/Like a return, yes*, and *Silenci, respostes, variacions/Silence, replies, variations*. A translator from English and French, he has been translated into Castilian, French, Czech and Chinese.

'Trofeu', in *Fins a un cert punt (Poesia 1945-1989)* (Barcelona: Edicions 62, 1989).

Joan Vinyoli, 1914–1984

Poet and translator. He published his first collection in 1937, in the middle of the Spanish Civil War. In 1948 he published a second volume of poetry in a semi-clandestine edition, but it was in the 1970s that his literary merit began to be recognised and that the most interesting part of his work was published — *Llibre d'amic/Book of the lover*, *Cercles/Circles*, *Passeig d'anniversari/Birthday walk*, and *Cant d'Abelone/Abelone's song*. The translator of Rainer Maria Rilke, Vinyoli's work is essentially a metaphysical reflection on existence. Taking a lucid and bitter standpoint, he believes that poetry alone is capable of transcending the reality of the passing of time and of death. He has been translated into Castilian and French, among other languages.

'Mar brut', in *Obra Poètica 1975-1979* (Barcelona: Ed crítica 1979). Also published in *Cercles* (Barcelona: Edicions 62, 1980), and in *Obra poètica completa* (Barcelona: Edicions 62, 2001).

Júlia Zabala, 1975–

A poet with a degree in Catalan philology from the University of Valencia, she teaches in a secondary school. Although her first published work was a volume of short stories, she is best known as a poet. Between 1995 and 2005 she published four books, of which three – *El mateix silenci/The same silence*, *Raïm de vent/Cluster of wind* and *El cercle de les ànimes/The circle of souls* – received literary awards. Her work, full of symbols which send us back to Arabic poetry, is a love song denouncing injustice, war and oppression. Her poems have been translated into Castilian and Russian.

'El teu nom gravat', in *Cendres volades* (Tarragona: El Mèdol, 2000).

For more information about these writers and about Catalan literature, see:

http://cultura.gencat.net/ilc/literaturacatalana800/index.html
http://cultura.gencat.net/ilc/qeq/
http://www.lletra.net/
http://www.escriptors.cat/autors.php

For more information about literary translations from Catalan, see:

http://www.llull.cat/llull/biblioteca/trac.jsp
http://www.pencatala.cat/ctdl/home/en

Translators' Biographies

Anna Crowe, 1945–

Born in Devonport, England, Anna Crowe was brought up in France and Sussex, and studied French and Spanish at the University of St Andrews. She has lived in St Andrews with her husband and three children since 1986. A prize-winning poet and translator, Anna Crowe teaches creative writing in schools and colleges and for the Arvon Foundation, and has led a poetry workshop for the Department of Continuing Education at St Andrews University for many years. In 1997 she co-founded StAnza, Scotland's poetry festival, and held the post of Artistic Director for its first seven years.

Her first poetry collection, *Skating Out of the House*, was published by Peterloo Press in 1997, and Peterloo has published her second full collection, *Punk with Dulcimer* (2006). Mariscat Press published her pamphlet collection *A Secret History of Rhubarb* in 2004. Her work, along with poems by Stewart Conn, was translated into Catalan and published as *L'Anima del Teixidor* (Edicions Proa, 2000) in a bilingual edition.

Anna Crowe's translation of Anna Aguilar-Amat's *Mùsia I Escorbut* was published on-line by Sandstone Press as *Music and Scurvy* in March 2005. She has also translated a collection by Joan Margarit, *Tugs in the Fog* (Bloodaxe Books, 2006), a Poetry Book Society Recommendation.

Christopher Whyte, 1952–

Born in Glasgow, Christopher Whyte has degrees from the universities of Cambridge, Perugia and Glasgow. From 1973 to 1985 he lived mostly in Rome. Between 1990 and 2005 he was first Lecturer and then Reader in the Department of Scottish Literature at Glasgow University. He now lives in Budapest, Hungary, and writes full time.

The author of four novels in English, and of the monograph *Modern Scottish Poetry* (Edinburgh University Press, 2004), he has also edited the anthology of 8 Gaelic poets *An Aghaidh na Sìorraidheachd* (Polygon, 1991) and *Dreuchd An Fhigheadair / The Weaver's Task; a Gaelic sampler* (Scottish Poetry Library, 2007).

His own Gaelic collections are *Uirsgeul / Myth* (Gairm, 1991), joint winner of a Saltire Award, and *An Tràth Duilich* (diehard, 2002). A third, *Dealbh Athar* will be published by Coiscéim (Dublin). His poems have appeared in translation in seven languages and he has translated poetry from a wide range of European languages into both English and Gaelic. See his website http://www.aboutchristopherwhyte.com

Acknowledgements

Our thanks are due to the following authors, publishers and heirs who have generously given permission to reproduce works:

poems by Montserrat Abelló, Anna Aguilar-Amat, Enric Casasses, Narcís Comadira, M. Josep Escrivà, Manuel Forcano, Feliu Formosa, Pere Gimferrer, Joan Margarit, Josep Palau i Fabre, Francesc Parcerisas, Teresa Pascual, Margalida Pons, Jaume Pont, Montserrat Rodés and Júlia Zabala are reprinted by permission of the authors;

poems by Agustí Bartra, Blai Bonet, Damià Huguet, M. Mercè Marçal, Miquel Martí i Pol and Joan Vinyoli are reprinted by permission of their heirs;

'Sonet sense retoc' by Joan Brossa from *Passat festes (1993-1995)* (Barcelona: Editorial Empúries, 1995) is reprinted by permission of Fundació Joan Brossa;

poems by Miquel Bauçà and Jordi Sarsanedas are reprinted by permission of Edicions 62.

Other XXV Anthologies

Intimate Expanses
XXV Scottish Poems 1978-2002

Edited by Ken Cockburn and Robyn Marsack

This anthology of 25 Scottish poems, one from each year from 1978 to 2002, presents an alternative view of how the past quarter century has unfolded in Scotland. These poems document history in small things as well as grand gestures, and range from sonnets and haiku to gargantuan list-poems.

The poets included are Iain Bamforth, Meg Bateman, John Burnside, Robert Crawford, Carol Ann Duffy, Douglas Dunn, Gerrie Fellows, Robin Fulton, Andrew Greig, George Campbell Hay, W.N. Herbert, Kathleen Jamie, Tom Leonard, Liz Lochhead, Norman MacCaig, Aonghas Macneacail, Kevin MacNeil, Edwin Morgan, Don Paterson, Richard Price, Seán Rafferty, Alastair Reid, Iain Crichton Smith, Alan Spence, Gael Turnbull.

'As this anthology begins in the year of MacDiarmid's death, it seems appropriate to open not with a poem by the old poet, but with a poem about the death of the father. Alastair Reid's touching, personal poem concludes not with an ending but a beginning, of "that hesitant conversation /which will go on and on". Indirectly all the writers of this quarter century are linked to MacDiarmid, in the sense that he provided the model of a poet questioning issues of identity, politics, culture, metaphysics and language within this shared geography which we call Scotland.'

from the Introduction by Ken Cockburn

ISBN 1 85754 795 0, December 2004, £7.95

At the End of the Broken Bridge
XXV Hungarian Poems 1978-2002

Edited by István Turczi and with an Introduction by Béla Pomogáts

István Turczi, with his wife Anna Palos Turczi, runs the publishing house Parnasszus, producing a quarterly literary magazine of the same name, as well books by contemporary Hungarian poets, translators and essayists. He is also a poet, novelist, dramatist and translator.

A number of poets in this volume will be familiar to Anglophone poetry-lovers, such as Ágnes Nemes Nagy, Ottó Orbán and Sándor Weöres, while others are being translated for the first time.

The poets included are István Baka, Zsófia Balla, Lászlo Benjamin, Győző Csorba, György Faludy, Győző Ferencz, Ágnes Gergely, Gyula Illyés, László Kálnoky, István Kemény, Endre Kukorelly, Lászlo Lator, Ágnes Nemes Nagy, Ottó Orbán, György Petri, Sándor Rákos, Zsuzsa Rakovszky, Zsuzsa Takács, Dezső Tandori, János Térey, Krisztina Tóth, István Turczi, Szabolcs Várady, István Vas, Sándor Weöres.

The poems have been translated into English and Scots by Ron Butlin, Tom Hubbard, Edwin Morgan, Angus Reid and Christopher Whyte. Zsuzsanna Varga has acted as literary consultant for the anthology.

'These twenty-five poems reflect the psychological history of those twenty-five years. They reflect the thoughts and feelings of Hungarian poetry about a historical period suffused with historical change. I am certain that the task of providing an authoritative picture of the history of a human community and a European nation is too important to be left to the hard (or even the softer) sciences alone: I believe it to be an important task of poetry. It is in this sense that the poems in the anthology can be seen to provide valuable and reliable insights into the mental and psychological history of Hungarians in the twentieth and twenty-first centuries.'

from the Introduction by Béla Pomogáts

ISBN 1 85754 796 9, April 2005, £7.95

How to Address the Fog
XXV Finnish Poems 1978-2002

Edited by Anni Sumari

This anthology of 25 Finnish poems, one from each year from 1978 to 2002, presents an alternative view of how the past quarter century has unfolded in Finland. 'I took it as my aim to make the selection as elegant (read: readable and suitably rough) and interesting as possible, rather than being faithful to "archaeological" layers – and that was all.' The poems include examples of Finnish modernism, prose poems, aphoristic pieces, and writing in Finland-Swedish.

The poets included are Kari Aronpuro, Bo Carpelan, Tua Forsström, Paavo Haavikko, Anne Hänninen, Hannu Helin, Markku Into, Eeva Kilpi, Eila Kivikk'aho, Juhani Koskinen, Jarkko Laine, Rakel Liehu, Arto Melleri, Lassi Nummi, Lauri Otonkoski, Markku Paasonen, Mirkka Rekola, Pentti Saarikoski, Helena Sinervo, Eira Stenberg, Anni Sumari, Arja Tiainen, Sirkka Turkka, Gösta Ågren; and the translators Donald Adamson, Robin Fulton and David McDuff.

'You have in your hands an anthology of Finnish poetry covering a period of 25 years (1978–2002). It begins with a wild prose poem experiment by Sirkka Turkka (b. 1939) – a text of four pages. Perhaps surprisingly, the prose poem is one of the central trends in contemporary Finnish poetry. It's a genre that has been practised intensively for several decades, yet typically its practitioners are often lyrical poets, not prose writers. One main reason for the strength of the prose poem may be the nature of the Finnish language: the words are relatively long, and numerous inflections are added on at the end of words. The language's very structure encourages both the prose poem and the long, prose-like stanza, which has recently been an equally strong stylistic genre. On the other hand, Finnish is adept at yielding neologisms whose associative and auditory qualities seem natural to the reader and are easily understood.'

from the Introduction by Anni Sumari

ISBN 1 85754 816 7, February 2005, £7.95

The Night Begins with a Question
XXV Austrian poems 1978-2002

Edited by Iain Galbraith

Whether Rilke or Celan, Hofmannsthal or Trakl, the writers who spring to mind when we think of modern German poetry were often Austrians – at least 'by formation'. Presenting 25 poems of the past quarter century this anthology brings the story up to date: "So Austrian, but at the same time so permeated by the whole world, and by the world surrounding this world", one of Thomas Bernhard's characters remarks of Ingeborg Bachmann's poem 'Bohemia, a Country by the Sea'. Something similar might be said of each of the poems in this compact and vital selection.

The poets included are Ilse Aichinger, Christoph Wilhelm Aigner, H. C. Artman, Ingeborg Bachman, Franz Joseph Czernin, Michael Donhauser, Oswald Egger, Franzobel, Erich Fried, Maja Haderlap, Ernst Jandl, Norbert C. Kaser, Marie-Thérèse Kerschbaumer, Alfred Kolleritsch, Friederike Mayröcker, Heidi Pataki, Reinhard Priessnitz, Andreas Okopenko, Peter Rosei, Robert Schindel, Evelyn Schlag, Ferdinand Schmatz, Raoul Schrott, Julian Schutting, Peter Waterhouse.

The poems have been translated into English and Scots by Iain Bamforth, Ron Butlin, Regi Claire, Ken Cockburn, Iain Galbraith and Angus Reid.

'If Scotland has been seen as a "nation without a state", then the Second Austrian Republic, it has been said, is "a state without a history", or – more attractively, if the nettle is grasped – with many histories. In one sense, then, its heritage of a diversity of fragmented, multicultural traditions might be thought to place modern Austria at the forefront of global developments ... But if post-war Austria has become an independent state, the people who live there cannot gain independence from Austria's several histories.'

From the Introduction by Iain Galbraith

ISBN 1 85754 915 5, February 2007, £8.95